DATE DUE

MR 9'91	DEC 11 '93	AUG 25	MR 26 07
MR 26'91	APR 8 '94	SEP 24	
AP 19'9	APR 28 '94	OCT 05	16 3
MY 2'9	JUN 20 '94	DEC 15	MY 24 '75
JE 15'91	JUL 19 '98	MR 20	E 24 '79
JY 9'9	AUG 15 '94	MR 10	
SE 9'91	JAN 31 '95	MY 11 '99	
OC 31'9	JUL 08 '9		
FE 25'92	AUG 26 '9	OC 14 '99	
SE 16'9	AUG 14 '9	DE 13 '99	
MR 8'9	OCT 21 '9	DE 14 '00	
NOV 28 '9	JAN 21 '9		

DEMCO

JUNIOR PET CARE

HAMSTERS

ZUZA VRBOVA

Photography Susan C. Miller
Hugh Nicholas
Illustration Robert McAulay
Reading and Child Psychology Consultant
Dr. David Lewis

ACKNOWLEDGMENTS

With special thanks to Jenny Toft, Bill Sayer, Mr. Hollingsworth, Photosound, Menor Photographic Services.

Library of Congress #89-52054

Distributed in the UNITED STATES by T.F.H. Publications, Inc., One T.F.H. Plaza, Neptune City, NJ 07753; in CANADA to the Pet Trade by H & L Pet Supplies Inc., 27 Kingston Crescent, Kitchener, Ontario N2B 2T6; Rolf C. Hagen Ltd., 3225 Sartelon Street, Montreal 382 Quebec; in CANADA to the Book Trade by Macmillan of Canada (A Division of Canada Publishing Corporation), 164 Commander Boulevard, Agincourt, Ontario M1S 3C7; in ENGLAND by T.F.H. Publications, The Spinney, Parklands, Portsmouth PO7 6AR; in AUSTRALIA AND THE SOUTH PACIFIC by T.F.H. (Australia) Pty. Ltd., Box 149, Brookvale 2100 N.S.W., Australia; in NEW ZEALAND by Ross Haines & Son, Ltd., 82 D Elizabeth Knox Place, Panmure, Auckland, New Zealand; in the PHILIPPINES by Bio-Research, 5 Lippay Street, San Lorenzo Village, Makati Rizal; in SOUTH AFRICA by Multipet Pty. Ltd., Box 235 New Germany, South Africa 3620. Published by T.F.H. Publications, Inc. Manufactured in the United States of America by T.F.H. Publications, Inc.

CONTENTS

NOTE TO PARENTS

A hamster is a simple and fun pet for a child to look after. *Hamsters* gently introduces children to caring for an animal and enjoying the commitment of having a pet. It is specially written for children of age 7 years and upwards in a lively way that encourages a child to understand the lifestyle of a hamster. Appreciating hamsters' natural habits forms an intrinsic part of their proper care. Just like children, all hamsters have different personalities. *Hamsters* is unique in that by providing a striking visual insight into a hamster's world, it promotes a happy and rewarding relationship between a hamster and its young owner.

YOU AND
YOUR HAMSTER

A hamster is a small, furry pet. It is small enough to fit into your cupped hands so that you can stroke it and play with it easily. After a while you will learn what your hamster likes and dislikes and, in the same way, your hamster will become used to you.

Syria is where many hamsters come from.

Hamsters are gentle animals but when you first buy your hamster, it may be a little shy and frightened. The more you play with your hamster, the more friendly your hamster will be toward you.

To make the most of having a hamster, it is important for you to learn about your hamster's ways and needs. Hamsters come from Syria. This is a hot and dry country in the Middle East. Pet hamsters have a very different way of life from their relatives and ancestors in the wild. But, their basic lifestyle—their eating and sleeping habits—is still similar to that of hamsters living in the wild.

Hamsters in the wild

In their natural desert home, hamsters sleep underground in their burrows during the day, and they only get up in the evening as the sun goes down. Animals that sleep during the day are called **nocturnal animals.** As pet hamsters sleep most of the day,

In the wild, hamsters sleep in burrows during the day and search for food at night.

you should try to be considerate of your hamster and not disturb it during the day if it is asleep. You can imagine how cross you would be if someone kept waking you up to play in the middle of the night.

In the desert, where they come from, hamsters roam around for long distances in search of food. Sometimes there is not very much food in the desert, and so hamsters are very sensible. When they find food they carry it back to their home burrows in pouches inside their mouths. They do not eat all their food right away but save some for later in case they cannot find food the next day. Pet hamsters do the same.

Hamsters often rub their face and body with their paws to clean themselves. They **groom** themselves like this, especially if they are nervous. It's a bit like someone scratching his head or playing with his hair. The hamster uses its front paws for washing. It licks them first and then washes its face.

As you most often see hamsters asleep during the day, at first you might think they are a little bit lazy. This is not at all true. You will soon notice that your hamster is very busy in the evening and at night. You will have lots of fun watching your active hamster friend running about in its cage, playing with the toys you provide, making and re-making its bed, grooming itself and playing games with you. Your hamster will be busy in its cage at night, just as it would be in the wild.

BUYING A HAMSTER

The ideal way of buying a hamster is to go to a pet store and choose one. The kind that you are most likely to see is the **Golden hamster** from Syria. It comes in various shades of brown and in white too. Golden hamsters vary a little in size but they are all small enough for you to hold easily in your hand. You can either buy one with long, shaggy fur or a short-haired one.

The Golden hamster has to be kept completely on its own, without any

Hamsters in a pet store. Notice that most of them are asleep during the day.

A young hamster in a pet store, ready to go to a new home.

other
hamster
companions in its cage.
If you try to keep more than
one hamster in a cage, they will fight
with each other and neither of them
will be safe.

You may think that your hamster
will be lonely on its own, but hamsters prefer to be kept on their own
because that is how they are used to
living. In the wild each hamster has
its own separate burrow.

If you do want to keep two hamsters together in one cage, it is best for you to buy **Russian hamsters.** They are available in some pet stores. Russian hamsters came originally from Russia and China. They are much smaller than Golden hamsters, so they are sometimes called **dwarf hamsters.** Sometimes they can even be called **hairy-footed hamsters.**

The age of your hamster

When hamsters are about six to eight weeks old, they are separated from their mother and brothers and sisters and taken to a cage of their own. It is best for you to buy a baby hamster, one about eight weeks old, so that it

Offer your hamster some food. This will help to relax it and get to know and trust you.

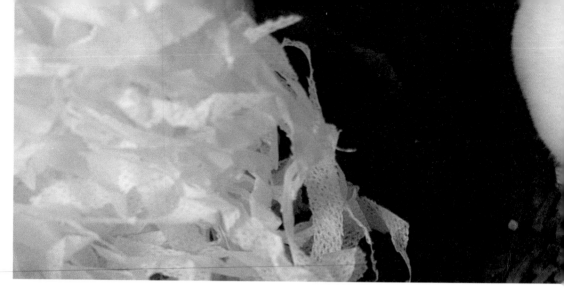

can get used to you when it is still a youngster. You will be able to tame your baby hamster yourself.

Your new baby hamster may be shy at first—just like you might be in a new home with people you did not know.

Making a choice

When you buy your hamster it is important for you to choose a healthy, good-natured one. Hamsters live for about two years, so it is an advantage if you pick one that will be fun and easy to look after all its life.

To do this you should try to look at the hamster you see in the pet store carefully. You can ask to look closely

at one you like by having it put on a table or the counter of the store. The hamster will be a little nervous at first.

A healthy hamster

First, look at the hamster's head carefully. Its nose should be clean and not runny. Its eyes should be clear and bright. Its ears should be sticking up firmly, clean and untorn. The teeth should be straight and undamaged. Then look at the hamster's body. The coat should be glossy and well-groomed because good, healthy hamsters like to groom themselves properly every evening. Make sure the hamster has no cuts or sore pat-

A hamster uses its forefeet to hold food and to help put food in and out of the pouch in its mouth.

ches on its body.

Finally, check the hamster's feet. They should be strong and sturdy, and the claws need to be short and trim and not split.

Try not to make any sudden moves as you are looking at the hamster, and give it a chance to get to know you. You could perhaps offer it a bit of food. Once it seems to be relaxed, you might like to gently stroke it. Hamsters have a good sense of smell, although they cannot see very well. Just letting the hamster sniff your finger will help it to get to know you.

Hamsters enjoy taking small pieces of food to a secret place in their nests.

A male or a female hamster

At the pet store, you may be asked if you would prefer a male or a female hamster. Both kinds make good, gentle pets, and it does not make any difference which you choose. But there is a chance that a young female hamster might have babies in the next few weeks after you have brought it home. This is something you should check with the person at the pet store.

Baby brother and sister hamsters are allowed to share the same cage until they are about 8 weeks old.

A HOME FOR YOUR HAMSTER

In the wild, a hamster lives underground where it builds nests and stores supplies of food. Hamsters like to hide their food from other animals in the desert that might try to steal it. The home that you provide for your hamster should have a place for the hamster to build a nest in and materials for building the nest. Then your hamster will be able to make itself comfortable.

There are plenty of different kinds of cages available in pet stores for you to choose from (below).

Your hamster's cage

Pet hamsters are usually kept in a cage, in a warm place indoors, away from drafts. Sometimes on a hot summer day you can take your hamster outdoors, in its cage, to give it some fresh air. If you do this, keep it out of the sun.

It is
best to
prepare
your
hamster's
cage and
make it as comfortable as possible
before you bring the hamster home.
First, place a layer of wood shavings in the cage. This makes a soft
floor for your hamster to walk on.
It has a similar feel to the soft,
warm sandy soil that your hamster
would burrow in out in the wild.

**Pieces of wood
are good for a
hamster to
gnaw on.**

Gnawing

Your hamster will appreciate a piece of wood from a tree placed in its cage. You might be able to find a small branch from an apple or pear tree in your backyard that your hamster will like to play with or chew on.

Your hamster's bed

Inside its cage the hamster will need some material to build its nest from. Hamsters like to snuggle down in their nests and go to sleep during the day. You can either give your hamster some fresh, dry hay to make its nest out of or buy some specially prepared nesting material from your pet shop.

The nesting material in your hamster's cage should be changed regularly.

Your hamster might prefer a mixture of materials to make a nest.

To make it more interesting for your hamster you can add to the mixture of nest-building materials by tearing up strips of tissue paper. At the end of the day you might see your hamster's sleepy head poking out from the warmth of its nest, getting ready to have some fun during the night.

Some materials that you might feel your hamster would like to make its nest out of, wool, for example, can be bad for your hamster. The hamster may swallow it, and it could cause a blockage in the hamster's tummy. It is better to be safe than sorry and buy the correct and safe nesting material from a pet store.

Toys for your hamster

Hamsters like to be busy and are playful animals. To prevent your hamster from becoming bored with its cage, give it some toys to play with. Hamsters like to scamper through the center of a cardboard tube and play with old thread spools, small jam jars and any other safe objects.

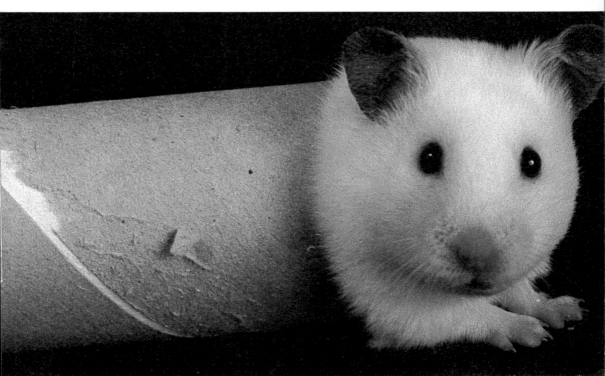

The need for exercise

Hamsters need exercise every day, just as we do. In the wild hamsters have lots of exercise because they travel long distances to find and collect their food.

As hamsters like to run about, it is best for your hamster if you equip the cage with a selection of ramps and ladders. Your hamster will enjoy scampering about and up and down on these. Putting exercise bars and shelves in the cage will enable your hamster to use every part of the cage, rather than just the floor space. The more like a play room your hamster's cage is, the more your hamster will enjoy it and feel at home in it.

An **exercise wheel** is an important part of a cage. Most hamsters like them and may spend hours on the exercise wheel, running many miles a day in it. It is fun to watch your hamster playing on its wheel.

Some hamsters, though, like their exercise wheels so much that they exhaust themselves on the wheel. It becomes a bad habit. If your hamster is one of those that runs on its wheel all the time, only leave the wheel in the cage for a few hours each evening.

As hamsters need to gnaw, it is best to buy a plastic or metal cage so that the hamster cannot gnaw through it and escape. Also, plastic and metal are easier to clean than wood.

FEEDING
YOUR HAMSTER

In the wild, hamsters mainly eat dry seeds which they find in the soil, but in some seasons they find green plants to eat. Pet hamsters are fortunate because they have a much wider choice of food than they would have in the wild. They eat almost anything you care to give them. They prefer hard foods like nuts and carrots because they can gnaw on them. Although hamsters like lots of different kinds of foods, they do not like sweets or chocolates. Even though you might like to give sweets to your hamster, remember that they are very dangerous because they could damage the inside of a hamster's mouth.

Hamsters like to eat sunflower seeds (right).

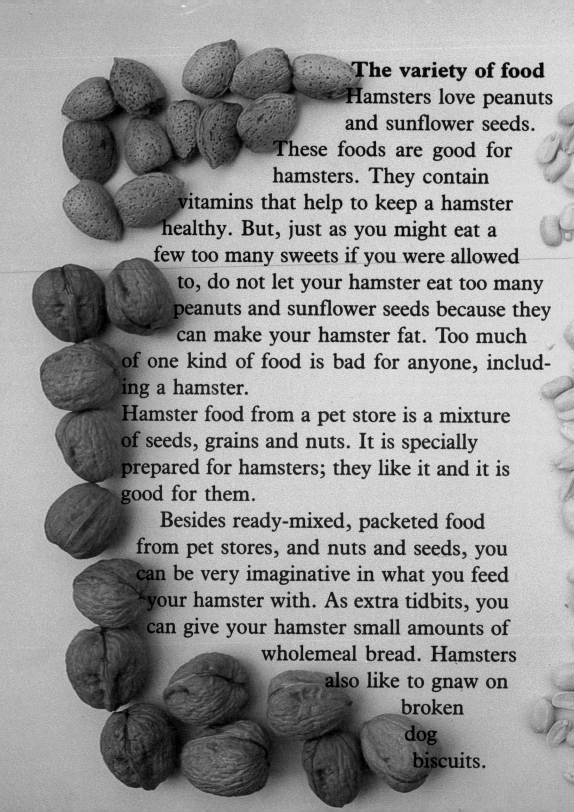

The variety of food

Hamsters love peanuts and sunflower seeds. These foods are good for hamsters. They contain vitamins that help to keep a hamster healthy. But, just as you might eat a few too many sweets if you were allowed to, do not let your hamster eat too many peanuts and sunflower seeds because they can make your hamster fat. Too much of one kind of food is bad for anyone, including a hamster.

Hamster food from a pet store is a mixture of seeds, grains and nuts. It is specially prepared for hamsters; they like it and it is good for them.

Besides ready-mixed, packeted food from pet stores, and nuts and seeds, you can be very imaginative in what you feed your hamster with. As extra tidbits, you can give your hamster small amounts of wholemeal bread. Hamsters also like to gnaw on broken dog biscuits.

Fruits and vegetables are also good
for your hamster. Your hamster
will like small pieces of lettuce or
cabbage, grapes and other fruits.
It is fun to give your
hamster tidbits and watch
it hold a piece of
food in its front
feet before it
scampers
away,
carrying it to a
secret hideout.

A hamster's hoarding habits

You will notice your hamster taking its food inside its nest and saving it there. Hamsters have special pouches in their cheeks to help them to carry food to different places and store it safely. In the desert a hamster would eat its food slowly in the safety of its burrow, where it cannot be attacked by another animal.

Pet hamsters like to do the same. They eat their food slowly, usually out of sight, hidden away in their nest.

The **pouch** is part of a hamster's mouth, formed by a fold of skin. It is like a special pocket that the hamster can fill up with food, using its front feet. The hamster can easily carry food to a safe spot and there unload the pocket full of food from its mouth.

Sometimes your hamster will fill its pouches up to the brim. You can give your hamster almost any kind of food that is good for you, to see if it likes it. Wild plants and flowers, such as dandelions and clover that you find in fields or in your backyard, are also good for your hamster. It is very important to your hamster to have some green food.

As hamsters store their food secretively, you will have to check that your hamster has not stored some fresh food in its nest that will go bad easily.

You can buy tasty treats—grain and seed cakes and sandwiches—for your hamster.

Food and water containers

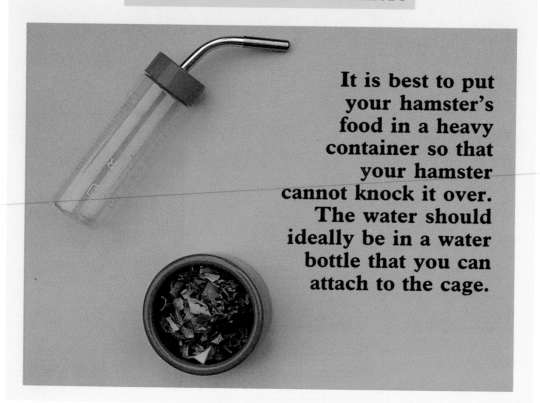

It is best to put your hamster's food in a heavy container so that your hamster cannot knock it over. The water should ideally be in a water bottle that you can attach to the cage.

Hamsters need to chew on hard things like wood or tough food like carrots—just like a baby likes to chew on a rattle or toy sometimes. It is good for your hamster to gnaw because this will keep its front teeth, the **incisors,** from growing too long. Unlike our teeth, a hamster's front teeth continue growing all through the hamster's life.

Hamsters need clean, fresh water every day.

HANDLING
YOUR HAMSTER

Hamsters are very shy animals. When you first bring your hamster home it might not seem to be very friendly towards you. Remember, it might not have been handled or even stroked at the pet store. It is up to you to help your hamster make friends with you.

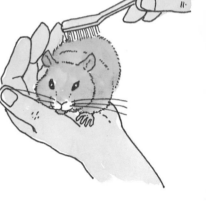

It might take you a few weeks to tame your hamster, and you will need to be very gentle and patient. If you suddenly try to cuddle your hamster on the first day you bring it home, it is quite likely to bite you.

Taming your hamster

Hamsters like the dark and they cannot see very well. They have a good sense of smell and they can hear your voice clearly. At first, just talk gently to your hamster each evening after you have given it some food. You can go on to place your hand in its cage, when it is playing, so that it gets used to your scent.

Hamsters are sensitive to scent and can recognize people by their different smells, although we cannot often do this. When your hamster has become used to your voice and scent, you can try to gently stroke it. To make sure you are not bitten, do not make sudden movements that will startle the hamster.

Gradually, your hamster will become friendly towards you, and after a while you will be able to pick it up and cuddle it every evening. If your hamster has been asleep all day, it will probably wake up to the sound of your coming home from school at the end of the day. It will be eagerly

How to Hold a Hamster Safely

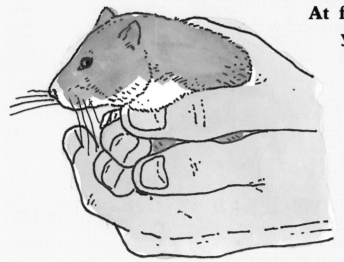

At first, it is best to keep your fingers away from the hamster's mouth in case it tries to nip you. Later on, when you have got used to each other, you will not need to be so careful.

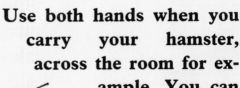

Use both hands when you carry your hamster, across the room for example. You can cup your hands into a bowl shape to give it a comfortable ride. If your hamster is hard to handle at first, it is because it is frightened.

waiting for you. Remember to be considerate. The golden rule is not to disturb a sleeping hamster.

Freedom to play

Some hamsters enjoy being allowed to roam about freely and to play in and explore a room indoors. If you let your hamster do this, you will have to watch it carefully, to make sure it does not escape, and keep the door of the room shut.

If you cannot catch the hamster after its playtime, try luring it into a bucket or jar with a carrot and cozy bedding material inside. You can then trap the hamster and put it back into its cage.

Like us, all hamsters are different, and some hamsters may not enjoy the freedom of a room. They may be frightened of the amount of space compared to the cozy cage and may try to hide.

GENERAL CARE

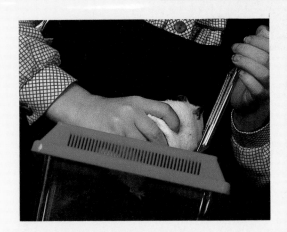 

When you clean your hamster's cage, you can put the hamster in a small animal container to make sure it is safe. You can buy these useful containers at most pet stores.

You can spray your hamster's cage to keep the bedding and woodshavings fresh (left).

It is fun to watch your hamster filling its pouches with food, grooming itself and playing in its cage. Besides watching, feeding and playing with your hamster, you will have to clean its cage. Hamsters are very clean animals and they do not smell.

A damp corner
You can put some wood shavings in a small, shallow container in your ham-

ster's cage and train your pet to use it as a toilet. This makes cleaning the cage an easy job for you to do every day.

All you will have to do is to empty the container. To toilet-train your hamster, each time you clean the cage leave some of the old, damp wood shavings in the small container. Hamsters are sensitive to scents and will soon realize that the container you have provided is supposed to be the toilet part of the cage.

The safest place to play with your hamster is on the floor. This way

It is a good idea to put your hamster in a play-ball, just for a little while, to keep it safe, while you are clean-ing the cage.

your hamster will not hurt itself if it suddenly jumps out of your hands. Hamsters can do this if they are surprised by a sudden movement or a loud noise. When you play with your hamster, keep a watchful eye on it all the time so that it does not escape.

Preventing an illness

Just like you, hamsters can catch colds, so if you have one it is best to keep away from your hamster for a few days until you are better. Otherwise, your hamster may catch your cold.

To make sure you do not catch an illness from your hamster, wash your hamster's food dishes and water bottle separately from the family's dishes.

In a deep sleep

Your hamster's cage should be in a place where the temperature is the same all the year round. At the beginning of winter, your house and the room you keep your hamster's cage in might become a little colder.

This is the time you should keep an especially watchful eye over your hamster, because some hamsters will curl up and go into a deep sleep for several weeks if they think it is going to stay cold. Going into a deep sleep

A cat will not realize that a hamster is your friendly pet and may well see it as a mouse to catch.

like this is called **hibernating.** We cannot hibernate, but some animals, for example, can do this naturally. It is a normal part of their lifestyle.

It is dangerous for a hamster to hibernate because it might not have sufficient stores of fat in its body to be able to stay alive, without eating, for several weeks. If your hamster looks as though it has gone into a deep sleep, do not try to wake it up. Simply place the cage in a warm room.

GLOSSARY

Dwarf hamster Another name for Russian hamsters which are typically much smaller than Golden hamsters.

Golden hamster The most common kind of hamster which is native to Syria and likes to live alone. It comes in brown and white, both in combinations and solids, and tends to be a little larger than the Russian hamster.

Grooming Hamsters are neat and clean animals all on their own, as they will clean, or groom, themselves at least once a day. You may, however, very gently stroke the hamster's coat with a soft toothbrush (not your own!).

Hairy-footed hamster Another name for the Russian hamster.

Hibernation In the wild, hamsters go into a deep sleep for the winter after having stored body fat all summer, spring and fall.

Incisors The hamster's front teeth which continue growing all its life. For this reason, it is important to provide something for the hamster to chew on.

Nocturnal animals Animals that are awake at night and sleep during the day.

Pouch A part of the hamster's mouth formed by a fold in the skin. The hamster fills it with food to transport home.